HERE ALL NIGHT

T0161029

10 9 8 7 6 5 4 3 2 1

Alice James Books are published by Alice James Poetry Cooperative, Inc., an affiliate of the University of Maine at Farmington.

Alice James Books
114 Prescott Street
Farmington, ME 04938
www.alicejamesbooks.org

Library of Congress Cataloging-in-Publication Data

Names: McDonough, Jill, author.
Title: Here all night / Jill McDonough.
Description: Farmington, Maine : Alice James Books, [2019]
Identifiers: LCCN 2019012581 (print) | LCCN 2019015654 (ebook) | ISBN
   9781948579582 (eBook) | ISBN 9781948579025 (pbk. : alk. paper)
Classification: LCC PS3613.C3885 (ebook) | LCC PS3613.C3885 A6 2019 (print) |
   DDC 811/.6--dc23
LC record available at https://lccn.loc.gov/2019012581

Alice James Books gratefully acknowledges support from individual donors, private foundations, the University of Maine at Farmington, the National Endowment for the Arts, and the Amazon Literary Partnership.

Cover photograph by Susan Mikula

HERE

POEMS

ALL

BY JILL MCDONOUGH

NIGHT

ALICE JAMES BOOKS
FARMINGTON, MAINE
ALICEJAMESBOOKS.ORG

CONTENTS

I

II

ACKNOWLEDGMENTS

2014 Pushcart Prize XXXVIII: Best of the Small Presses (2014 Edition): "Ming"

The Adroit Journal: "It's What You Said You Wanted"

AGNI: "What's New"

The Baffler: "Do What You Love"

The Baltimore Review: "Enchantment"

Bird's Thumb: "What the Boyfriends Teach Us"

The Boston Globe: "Dr. Li Shovels!"

Common-place: "Satan's Cupboard"

CONSEQUENCE: "But Yet"

The Drum: "Also, Homemade Flamethrowers"

Drunk Monkeys: "That's My Taco: A Villanelle for Jim Rockford" and "ROOM FOR PARTY"

Fugue: "Fawn Bleat" and "Happy"

Gulf Coast: "Late Leeks"

Hanging Loose: "Sealing Woodrow"

Hobart: "Casual Sleep," "Man's Man," and "Still Falling"

Let the Bucket Down: "Woman Comes into the Bar"

Love's Executive Order: "Sewn Stripes, Embroidered Stars"

A Mighty Room: A Collection of Poems Written in Emily Dickinson's Bedroom: "Emily
  Dickison, Amazonian Canoes"

Memorious: "Another Art"

Pangyrus: "For I Will Consider My Friend Susan"

Plume: "The Women in the Shoe Store Ads Are All in Love with Each Other, but Not Really
  They Are in Love with Shoes Thousands of Shoes"

Poem-a-Day: "Our Father"

Salamander: "I Don't Know Greek," "Lundi Gras at Commander's Palace"

The Shallow Ends: "Bruegel"

Southern Indiana Review: "On Faculty Meetings"

Radical Teacher: "Cindy Comes to Hear Me Read" and "Gay Freaking Assholes: On Tolerance"

Talking River: "My Body Is a Temple" and "I Dream of God in Oxford"

The Threepenny Review: "Ming," "Sonnet for the Money," "In Which I Am Accused of Sleeping
  My Way to the Top," and "Ferris Wheel's a Ship"

THRUSH: "Poor Pussy"

Unsplendid: "Hot Dogs, Fresh Buns: Tetrameter for Dre" and "Tuesday Morning"

Viator: "I *Said*—" and "The HPV Sonnets"

These poems were written with support from a Lannan Literary Fellowship, a Wallace Stegner
Fellowship at Stanford University, the Dorothy and Lewis B. Cullman Center for Scholars and
Writers at the New York Public Library, a Visiting Artist Residency at the Am erican Academy in
Rome, a Visiting Writer position at Westminster College, and a Joseph P. Healey Research Grant
from the University of Massachusetts Boston. Thank you.

DO WHAT YOU LOVE

Do what you love, they said. The money
will follow, they said. They didn't say what
the money should follow, or who. Poor money, lost
money: money must have been so much confuse!
One money, twice, eleven monies, four: money trying
to keep it together, ragged flock of nonnative stragglers,
lollygaggers, each losing its buddy, special follow-time
friend. Money talks, but not like I do. Poor monies, mute
ESL-speaking lost souls. Do what you love and the money
will follow. Until it gets distracted, follows somebody else!
Until love doubles back, shrugs money off its trail. Money
follows love like good money after bad. Bad money!
Mad money, bad habits, dying hard. Do what you love,
they said, but what if what you love is watching *Die Hard*
for the dozenth time? When maybe you can't sleep?
Look at poor Bruce Willis's poor bloody feet: pause
it there, make popcorn with nutritional yeast,
talk about how there must be some sneakers
somewhere in that building. But no. Alas! There wasn't
any time. No time for shoes? Baby needs a new pair
of shoes; *mama don't work for free*, Sandra says. Time
is money, they said, and you are profligate, spendthrift,
a lazy-ass wastrel, leaning in doorways, on bars, leaning back
on Wright's hammock, again and again. Again. Lolling,
lollygagging, shrugging when they *I know you must be
very busy*, grinning when they sigh how busy they are.
Busy! Not so much! Because you do you, baby; keep
doing what you love: nothing. *Nothing that is not there
and the nothing that is* oh, nothing. Nothing much.

MING

That's why we don't keep things in stairwells.
—Mary Warnement, The Boston Athenaeum

When the former curator remembers the Ming,
remembers knocking it over, he remarks, "the thing

took fucking forever to fall." Shaking
his heavy head. Inside, the Ming's still taking

its time. Still falling. Look: he opened the magic door,
invented a way of making more

time. All of us always longing for longer, a few extra hot
days in July, sunshine, more time with the kids. Not

this endless loop, cringing eternity, fucking forever in the poor
guy's vase-sized head. Scott asks if I'd be twenty again. *Not for*

all the money in the world. But then I sort of take
it back, bargain: Would I for sure meet Josey? Could I bank

the money I did not give back to the world—just Jeter's share,
net worth of the board of Goldman Sachs—relive those years

and then have the rest of my life with her, her and fewer
jobs? A car, dishwasher, dryer. New roof, newer

shoes, Josey's never-swollen one-shift-a-week knees.
Go back to twenty, to the instant the Ming first leans

into thinner air. This vase makes it through Bruegel,
the new world, microscopes. From bustles to Google

to finally fall. But not finally anything: always it slips

from a half-hearted shelf, fresh from its crated straw, his fingertips

always in reach. You gain a week, say, week of replay, your fault
in the space-time continuum, week of stutter and halt

taken back in slivers of seconds, in panicked gasps, sleep rent
again. You gain a week. This is how it's spent.

FAWN BLEAT

Linda dabs on Pure Earth smell and waits in a blind,
whispers what to do once you shoot a porcupine.

One was *the size of a baby seal*, its chubby corpse
a five-buzzard one. Undertaker beetles, black and orange,

live in dead animal bodies, invisible to us. Problem solved.
We look online for perfect calls to imitate: Rabbit Screaming, Fawn

in Distress, Rabbit in Distress—Rabbit in Distress? It drives us
<u>crazy</u>. *I need to hear that again*, Josey says, while the rest of us

cringe and moan. *I dated him in high school*,
Rachel says. Linda tried out her Fawn Bleat call

by suggesting her friend try it at Mary Baker Eddy's
coyote-haunted grave. Why not? We make the Fawn Bleat

so many times—Michael is terrific at it, Michael Kusek
is the best—Susan and Rachel send me a whole set:

Death Chamber Grunt Call. Witchy Woman. Squirrel, or
Wet Willy Box Call. And finally, my favorite: Squawler.

STILL FALLING

My friend's trying to stop smoking, and I say Oh cut yourself some slack, sick
of pretending we're not going to die. We are going to die still falling

for crap about berries, a glass of red wine. It could be worse. We're not suicidal,
smack fiends, Swazi. So we're still skipping the gym, still eating fries, still falling

to sleep with the TV on. Whatever. We're daily closer to dying, but
it appears to happen slow. Nightfall, dusty snow, cold night still falling,

he laughs, long rope of smoke, warm breath rising. *Right. We each
hang ourselves, but it's a long rope, Jill.* See? We're all still fine, still falling.

LUNDI GRAS AT COMMANDER'S PALACE

For Billy, Nikki, Josey, Rosie, and Pearl

We drink good whiskey under the magnolia trees,
talk about how the dead can't see how great
life gets. What a rip! All the happinesses we
couldn't have imagined, growing up. Next day,
dressed up, we walk to our long-held reservation, see
the jealous tourists point. The jazz trio
makes me and Josey cry: milk punch, so little sleep,
and also we're just saps. Billy requests "I Can't Give You
Anything but Love," so our tears gleam a while, stream
through *that's the only thing I've plenty of.*
Our serenader lies, baby, and we laugh at how we
cry at plenty, friendship, death, foil crowns, love
him, him confused. He sees my tears and pats
my back: *Now what on earth could be sad about that?*

WHAT THE BOYFRIENDS TEACH US

Susan's boyfriend made a list, so at the store
he'd remember to buy more *ice cubs*.
The algorithm won't let this happen anymore.
It knows if you are sleeping; it knows if you are dumb.

It knows if you've been bad and want offers from busty
adulterers, hushed hotel suites in Montreal.
When I text *its* the phone knows when to apostrophe.
The phone's always right. I barely need to spell.

The strangers who wrote the algorithm help
me every day: invisible guardian angels who turn
fuck to *duck*, try to help me be some better self.
I learned *it's* from *its* when I was nineteen, burned

when a college boyfriend corrected my flirty,
wrong emails. Once I got a note in junior high,
an apology, tucked in yellow and purple grocery
store mums. Polo cologne-scented page, torn right

out of a spiral notebook, college ruled: *Dear Jill*,
it read, in childish cursive: *I've been such a fuel.*

BUT YET

That summer poetry class at the university I said over
and over to knock it off with *but yet*. It was their most
pointed transition statement. They said it so often, imbued
with such heft, I started to love it. I warned them about this
friction: *I know you're serious. But yet I laugh.*

One cried once. Not because I'm a jerk, not because *but
yet*. He was reading his poem on PTSD, or trying.
Next thing you know he's trying to get his shit
together while we all hold very still. Just there
with the chill of chalkboards, cement blocks. All on his side.
On the first day, he said since he got back sometimes
he just tears up, so don't freak out if he does.

So when we see him crumple, I say *Okay,
let's take ten minutes*, take him outside to stand
in the sun while he hitches *I'm sorry*s, tries to take
a decent breath. It's not in my lesson plan
but I pull him to me, hold his big body
in my arms, saying *shh* until he can stop
sobbing. Then I squeeze quick, say *You trying to get
me fired?* and he laughs. I step back, say *So not
appropriate*, and he's better. For now. But yet.

CASUAL SLEEP

I dream we're all so tired all
the time we start watching strangers
sleep. Videos of people asleep
all snuggled up in flannel, under down.

Sleep-tastic grow the YouTube channels.
Mattress stores tuck sleepers in their tidy
cotton beds. A cottage industry yawns
open: major in Sleep, become a Sleep Coach.

Commodity, new field: *I was in finance but now
I'm in sleep*. Sleepers in shop windows wrapped
in fleece, conked out on couches. Subway riders
scroll through sleepers on their smartphones,

brushing sleep from dreamers' eyes with thumbs.
On Craigslist, "Strictly Platonic," one man's
an *open-minded* expert, can sleep *for days*,
his listing says. He can sleep *through literally anything*.

He lists his bicep's circumference, the height his shoulder
could heft or nestle your heavy head. *The best
sleep of your life*, he promises, next to a photo of him
in crisp, sky-blue pajamas. Brushing his perfect teeth.

THAT'S MY TACO: A VILLANELLE FOR JIM ROCKFORD

I just want to watch some goddamn *Rockford Files*:
cute ladies wear slacks; the bad guys chew gum.
Maybe after this I'll watch some *Magnum, P. I.*

I love the snappy dialogue: "He's in the joint."
"That's my taco!" "Stay here; I'll check it out!"
I just want to watch some goddamn *Rockford Files*.

I'll have more soup; fifth fucking bowl today.
If I cough anymore I'm going to piss myself.
Maybe after this I'll watch some *Magnum, P. I.*

I should take a bath with eucalyptus oil, sea salt,
go back to bed with some herbal tea, but
I just want to watch more goddamn *Rockford Files*.

I love the theme song, trailer, Firebird that never dies.
He climbs out wincing, has a hitch in his get-along.
Maybe after this I'll watch some *Magnum, P. I.*,

but I hate the sensitive voice-over; compared to Jim
Rockford, Magnum's kind of gay. What's up with those shorts?
I just want to watch some goddamn *Rockford Files*,
but I guess I can settle for some *Magnum, P. I.*

WHITEY BULGES

Josey's driving our Subaru, which we have because
we're lesbians, because the butch one usually drives.

Although we're both great drivers, and we're vain
about the Subaru being stick. Anyway, she's driving, and I

read friends' texts out loud. I tap her shoulder with the back
of my hand to indicate where one ends, another starts.

Like a slash when quoting poetry in prose to indicate
a line break, or the man in front at church who marks

time like a conductor sans baton. For instance *We
have simple syrup* (tap) *and grenadine* (tap). *"Whitey*

Bulges" would be a good porn name, I tell her, out of nowhere.
I want to get Heidi in there somehow, for Whitey's hiding.

Maybe Whitey's girlfriend could use it, the one
with her teeth cleaned once a month: Heidi Whitey Bulges.

But really any white stripper in the greater Boston
area could use it. You could. Go ahead. I don't mind.

I DON'T KNOW GREEK

but I know what I like, I think, when the kid admits
I don't know Greek, looking down at the Latin
on the page. Two minutes in a still classroom they want
to stretch out to twenty, absorbed in the new
sets of blocks I've given them, the sound and stress,
a way to pay attention, a way to make
their writing sound good to them. Sudden unveiling,
freedom of form. The mind, distracted by iambs,
getting out of its own damn way for once.
You can do anything in meter. You
can forget the dough on the stove top, let it rise
and sour, then bake it, fill the house with steam,
the pioneer scent of fresh baked bread. You can
conjure a fur hat, a silver necklace,
surprise gifts in small boxes on the bed.
Notes on the kitchen table, haloed clouds
meringue impossible above the bay.

IT'S WHAT YOU SAID YOU WANTED

I think it's a poem. I think I wrote it down. Andrea

calls. We talk for an hour and then she says she thinks

she wrote a poem. *I think it has a title.* She takes

the phone downstairs—footsteps, shifting handset. She finds

the book—*I hope I can read my writing*—and then reads

—her voice gentle, low, an excellent thing in a woman—

You don't have to ask about the odds, they're

stacked against you like cordwood, like—oh, wait. No.

I'm sorry. This isn't it. I thought it was a poem but it's not.

I SAID—

I blame you for what I have become.
Spoiled for choice, for good; quilled mums
in the garden, mowing leaves into mulch
come fall. *She bring you coffee in your
favorite cup?* Reason enough to stay over,
stall. Humdrum. Same old. Everyday
new with you, you guys. Texts punctuated
with silence, with digital beats. *You've
done everything just right.* What's the secret
of comedy? Not emoticons. The Lucky
Star to Chinatown, free wifi, free
busmates muttering in a thousand
tongues. Susan calling to ask if she can
wear Dre's dress. *What are you birds doing?*
Walking to Jane Street strapped into bags. Then
river views, Lackawanna Erie, police boats, light
on the water, pilings by the shore. Escargot
when you want it, oysters when you don't.
NO, baby, NO, don't do it! Xmas Eve
Pats tix. Only her creditors know
for sure. When a guard shouts at me
when I'm teaching in prison, I confess that I'm
not used to it, tell my students, the way I live? No one
tells me what to do. We all sit still a second
with that wonder: then *Dag. She said
nobody tells her what to do.*

THE HPV SONNETS

We say so much good stuff we write it down
on the table, take the table's paper when
we leave. *Yale'll pay good money for that*
shit, I tell them. This is a joke about
being a Famous American Poet which sorry
but no such thing. Also an excuse
to invent and use "*Yale'll*." A sunny day
in June at Odeon, Sancerre outside with steak
tartare, my BLT. Rosie, Melanie, and me
on Michael Douglas's HPV, Melanie's dad,
who says *don't go to the doctor unless your eyes*
are pussing blood. The man's a doctor.
Pus we like so much we laugh so hard
that we get *Pus the Magic Dragon, Pus*
in fucking Boots. In other news, to *pus?*
A verb. A verb for blood. We love pus: its
one s, that it's disgusting, almost but not quite
obscene. Melanie finds out that I'm a poet,
regrets the lowbrow shit she's said, so Rosie
reassures her: *She's got pus in all*
her poems. Blood and pus and glory, gore
a sort of coded language saying *you*
can trust me. I'm here to have
a good time. We're here for hours, days
and years of this if we're that lucky. Thank
God. Thank you. We'll be here all night.

FOR I WILL CONSIDER MY FRIEND SUSAN

For she is the servant of the Living God,
and worships in her way. For this is done
by wiping her Countertops seven times over
with evident Quickness. For she worries
and plans, asks me to cut Onions for supper
in a Quarter-Inch Dice. For her concerns
are so evident on her face I am even willing
to cut Onions in a Quarter-Inch Dice. For this
she loves me, for she knows it is not of my Nature
to be precise, to bring precision to any first
draft, which is living, which is cutting up foods
to be consumed for suppertime. For she is a mixture
of Gravity and Waggery, and even in her precision
finds a way to treasure me, though my sloppy little
spirit is such a Challenge to love: I forget my
toothbrush, forget my Pants, drink all the Gin,
leave coffee rings, make more reasons to wipe
more Counters more times. For there is nothing
sweeter than her Peace when at rest, after two
gin and tonics on the green velvet sofa with a Stringle,
pretzels, in front of a vintage *Antiques Roadshow.*

THIS NEXT POEM

This next poem reflects a…twisting journey,
a series of…encounters with transcendence,
a struggle with the big picture, with meaning.
It asks difficult questions, choreographs
complicated answers in a kind of…*trance*.
I was working on it over a summer spent
on a feminist organic farming collective in France,
and I'd like to thank my friend Delphine, who lent
me the gloves I mention in the third stanza. In
the last couplet I construct a…collage of words
by Catullus, Jorie Graham, and Loretta Lynn.
I doubt you'll recognize their voices merged
in this…sort of *flamenco*, "burning on the page."
It's called "Flamenco: Burning on the Page."

HOT DOGS, FRESH BUNS: TETRAMETER FOR DRE

For walking around the fire pit, around
the genius of Slip 'N Slide, banked sides.
For its lessons in physics, wonder, guts,
half-pipe slick and rising, stripped down
and catching air. For gratitude
for a tray of perfectly charred hot dogs
tucked in their soft fresh buns. Grown-ups
in groups, laughing in the dark.
Visible tips of lit joints, lit shared
cigarettes, various stages of
undress. Unless the punch. Unless the stars,
all practically shooting. Splash pool unseen,
just audible at the end of slide.
For the dark. For the laughing silhouettes
by the pop and rustling bonfire down
the carved, smart-plasticked hill. For drunk,
delighted grown-ups; hot dogs! Hot dogs
in buns to save their lives on such
a night. Such a summer in Western
Mass, soft mass of stars and breezes.
For the people, the Cheetos, trampoline.

SHORE LEAVE, SOUTH BOSTON

When Josey waits on the Portuguese Tall Ship seamen
and the local girls they just picked up, they order

Long Island Iced Teas. Josey loves them anyway, their adorable
accents, dress whites, quick success with the ladies.

So she takes out the four white spirits, talks about how
each can shine: Vodka with caviar and blini; gin

with its cardamom, black pepper spice; tequila, straight with sangrita;
Hemingway daiquiri rum. But together, she tells them, blunted

with triple sec, Coke, *what's the fucking point*. They love her, take her up
on Hearsts and Aqueducts, give her an enameled Tall Ship pin.

They want to take the girls back, lucky girls, cook for them
in the galley. *What is this thing*, one asks Josey, *this small*

thing it comes with martinis. When she tells him he cries out
Olives! I will cook for you cod with olives. One girl

makes a face, says *it's too late to eat* but the other kicks her
under the bartop, says *I'm starving. I think that sounds great.*

HAPPY

We can make each other happy, Harry Nilsson screams
from our speakers, and I say, *Oh, Harry: no we can't.*
We turn it up, drive up the coast with the windows
down, sing every part, even the wack-ass *Whoa-oa-oa
-oa-oh!*s. I had never heard of Harry Nilsson, being
younger than Josey, a fact I mention as often as I can.
Like me, it never gets old. So I knew all the songs,
didn't know they were all by one guy. This makes me
happy, makes me remember, or invent, a babysitter
who played this tape in her black Trans Am, wore
feathered roach clips in her black feathered hair.
Probably now she's Josey's age. *We were happy then*,
we sigh sadly, when we hear ourselves remember
anything out loud. Remember when we caught all
those mackerel in the harbor, saw a hundred seals?
My two men from Cameroon, your guy on Flexeril?
You didn't know where you started, where I began.
Too broke to go to the movies, we biked a Bustelo can
of coins over there. The ladies' room at the Meow Mix!
The Independent, election day! The Swedish doctor brought
her perfect breasts to your house and said she loved you.
You said you didn't care. *We were happy then*, we say, making
each other so happy, trying and failing to keep a straight face.

TUESDAY MORNING

I see you. From the bed we built up high,
above the dusty winter clothes, red shoes.
Under quilts and comforters you hogged last night,
I see you're rushing: the edger's thirty-two
extra if it's not back by eight at Rent-
A-Center, Watertown. Past the doorjamb,
in the kitchen, your elbow's bright, intent
on sawing bread, spreading cream cheese and jam.
You move from sink to fridge, hips static, trim
and swiveling to drawers for waxed paper: who
uses waxed paper anymore? You bring
me coffee, kiss me goodbye again. You—
who would believe it?—have foamed the milk. You
smile, slide the drawers, press the fridge door to.

ALSO, HOMEMADE FLAMETHROWERS

In my zombie movie, zombies figure out the humans are in the food courts.

In my zombie movie, survivors are holed up in libraries, reading up on how to keep their people safe and fed.

My zombie movie has passages in which we see the handwriting of a troubled writer, creamy pages filling in hissing propane light.

In my zombie movie, the smart zombies evolve to discover that the more challenging, more delicious humans hole up in libraries.

In my zombie movie, over several scenes, the creamy pages add up. The writing becomes richer, more beautiful. Demonstrating the gradual passage of time.

In some ways my zombie movie is like *Frankenstein*, if the monster ate people and had a lot of friends.

Spoiler alert for my zombie movie: our writer is the first sentient zombie.

I dreamed my zombie movie. In the end, we survivors were in a safe house with hella locked doors. I saw new people approach in clean Carhartts, white coats. With hard hats, clipboards, and briefcases.

And I called out to my fellow humans, *Look at them smiling! Look how clean, how reassuring! Plus which it's daytime!*

So we opened the door.

ENCHANTMENT

We're in Eberswalde, where they burned
the synagogue on Kristallnacht, where Ravensbrück
had a subcamp. After the war the East made it into
a club. A perfectly good building; why tear it down?
Before the band plays we walk through, beyond
the Christmas-lit bar, bright stage, to a dark room
of upturned leather club chairs: I think
of lampshades made of human skin.
Darker corridors and doorways, sunken
cardboard boxes, moldy overhead projector.
The doors are heavy. Concrete absorbs
all sound, though we're only rooms away
from the DJ, dancers, happy hour.
In one room we find thirteen sewing machines,
oak tables. I imagine they're the women,
under some enchantment. Freed from body,
breath, made into this, and we're come here
to save them. The music starts at ten.
Kids who come to see the show have shaved heads,
drab jackets, combat boots, tattoos. *I'm through*,
I'm thinking, want to fly home, cart off
the sewing machines. Scrub one sewing machine
with brushes, steel wool, Murphy's Oil Soap.
Rub warmed linseed oil in the table's thirsty grain,
let oak, enamel rest, soak it in on sheets of Sunday's
New York Times. The stoves are lit for hours,
but we still see our breath. The whitewash, disco
balls, and colored lights are new, but it was cold like this
for them. Our visible breath historically accurate.
We are burning all the coal we want.

I THINK YOU WILL BE ABLE TO HUG HER

— Rio Bennin talking to Peter Lee on *This American Life*

The i-limb ultra from Touch Bionics, new *robot hand*,
how it moves, makes me look at my hands like I'm
on acid, filled with the glory of the God of our Hands.

Pick up a water bottle: *double contraction*, wrist spinning
Exorcist-style. We hear the wrist spin in the background,
hear both men laugh. *I think that you can pick an egg up*

with it. I've seen people do it. He looks at himself
in a mirror: *It's pretty wild…a carbon fiber pattern*
on the forearm, and then this kind of translucent white glove

over a black robotic hand. And it really looks cyborg.
They decide he will probably be able to hug his girlfriend:
Yeah, it will probably be one of the first things we try.

CINDY COMES TO HEAR ME READ

Cindy: not her real name. I met her
in prison, and people in prison I give
the fake names. I taught her Shakespeare, remember
her frown, wide eyes, terror of getting
things wrong. Her clear, arguable thesis
on Desdemona's motives, Desdemona's past. The last
days were hard on her, it taking visible work
to see things could be worse. Imagine: I did.
But now she's out! In jewelry and makeup, new
clothes, haircut she chose and paid for. We hugged.
We'd never hugged; it's not allowed. On the outside
you can hug whoever you want. She told me she has
an apartment now, a *window*, an ocean view. She has
a *car*, she told me, and we both cracked up. The thought of it
wild, as farfetched then as when you're a kid playing
grown-up, playing any kind of house. She has
a job. She drives there in traffic. Each day
she sees the angry people. Sweet, silly people,
mad—God bless them—at traffic. At other *cars*.
She laughs, she told me, laughs out loud alone
in her car. People around her angry as toddlers. Whole
highways of traffic, everybody at the work of being free.

ON FACULTY MEETINGS

I don't want to be repetitive here, but just
to highlight some concerns the others have
been raising... here's the kind of thing I bust
my pen out for in meetings. Just no. Just pave
the way. Just walk on by. Just don't. No *I*
just wanted to say or *I just wanted to bounce*
off something she said or *just to reiterate.* Why
justify ourselves, just think of how
all this might work. *Just a smidge,* okay, *just wait*
a sec, justs taking more time than the thing we want
to say. We reach as high as we can, raise
our hands toward the glory of being called on,
then back off with *just.* Just take it, hon. Just drink
it up. You have our attention. Just say what you think.

EMILY DICKINSON, AMAZONIAN CANOES

I get to write in Emily Dickinson's bedroom,
dine out on her tiny desk, joke if they gave
the girl a bigger desk, she could've been writing
novels. *What a waste.* Bob and Deborah
love this, help me pronounce *vent-a-vol.*
Vol-au-vent. Something. It's chicken. Very
good. Susan says *Poor Emily*; *one trestle table away
from War and Peace.* Laughing like this
at a table like this—dappled summer shade, tall
cherry trees—is all I ever wanted when I didn't know
what one could want. As a child I wanted to be
a prostitute or lounge singer, understood from TV this
meant cocktails, fur coats, satin. Laughing grown-up
friends like Jim Rockford, plus cool neon signs.
Bob ate chicken *vol-au-vent*—*A recipe
from my childhood*, he says. Susan says *My childhood
was very different from yours*. And I say *Mine, too*,
ask if he's had Lean Cuisine, or Chef Boy-Ar-Dee ravioli,
cold from the can. But I have read a lot, know
that like beef Wellington, the pastry's lined
with *duxelles*. *Ducks-Ells* I say, and he helps me
say *do-sell*, because it's French. This is the problem
when you read more than you talk, or, anyway, more
than you listen. As a child I told my dad I loved
seeing water meet the *WHORE-is-on*, having read
horizon, never heard it before. Maggie asked
her prof what Robert Frost meant by *belly-laced*.
Belilaced, Ann Winters sighed. We eat *vol-au-vent*
at the kind of place where they put a plate of food in front
of you, come back with a silver pitcher, pour more
foods on the food that you've got. The patio looks
like the Eiffel Tower's ironwork. The Eiffel Tower's

ironwork's based on a Regina Victoria lily, Bob tells us,
leaf structure supporting enormous flowers.
He saw them from a canoe in the Amazon.
If I had a nickel for every time I was in a canoe
in the Amazon, I say, *Bob, I'd be nickel-free.*

I DREAM OF GOD IN OXFORD

God and I walk the cobbled streets and courtyards
together. Me, walking with God, sometimes
with Christ. I tell Him I won a fellowship at Stanford—
He looks at me like *duh*, like He didn't know—and
that I will need a part-time job. Apparently I think
a stroll around a medieval town with God
is a good opportunity for networking. But God
lets me down. He summarizes His CV; when he talks
firmament, Adam and Eve, old testament stuff, He's huge,
a Macy's Thanksgiving Day Parade balloon tethered
beside me. Flowing robes, giant sandals, floating.
When He reminds me of His stints in corporeal form,
He's regular again, guy-size, companionable Christ
in Oxford, skimming past the New Library, Old
Ashmolean, Eagle and Child, The King's Arms.
And so our Lord reminds me how His occasional physical
jobs—swan or golden shower, Christ on a cross—
helped Him further His real work. God is advising me
to get work as a gardener, or prep cook, work where
my body, lifting, toting, is what's of use.

I wake up and think it over: God, I decide,
has forgotten—He hasn't been manifest in years—
that stuff pays for shit. I was hoping
He'd suggest a place at Google, hook me up
with something, maybe as a paralegal. God
as good intentions, clueless as a guidance counselor.
God a little high and mighty, as if I don't know
carpentry and gardening are noble callings. God
all wrong, but charming. Good company, nonetheless.

MY BODY IS A TEMPLE

I hear some guy say and I think yeah: no shoes
allowed in here. Once a friend said *You treat
your body like an amusement park*, made me
proud. The body as house: *This House We Live In*,
the skull its cupola, your mouth the front door.
The world's oldest temple is in Urfa, the *New
Yorker* tells me. Elif Batuman writes
it's eleven thousand years old. The pillars look
like people: their temple was a body. They hold
hands, wear loincloths, necklaces. Gobekli Tepe:
don't you want to go there? Here
is a list of the animal bones she says they've
found: *leopards, goitered gazelles, wild
cattle, wild boars, red deer, foxes, cranes,
and vultures*. My body is not an amusement park:
it's that temple, which loves the body, dear organs
slogging along in a sifting age of trash. Bless
your liver, heart, your lungs, hand-holding pillar.
You are a miracle, Noah's ark, filled
with scorpions and vultures, the poor
goitered sweet gazelle. Companion, blessed
event. Body as snowstorm, unrealized
ecstasy. A whole history of man.

ANOTHER ART

The art of finding isn't hard to master,
either. We find so many things, past or

present. Your way home. Yourself. In a pickle,
a jam. Find something every day: steel bristle

from the street cleaning truck, lucky penny
on the ground. Then practice finding many,

finding more: ten dollars in your winter coat, a stolen
hour, lunch with this woman you love. The pollen

from stargazers staining her shirt.
In the wine, find *stone fruit, ash.* Share the dessert.

Find a volunteer melon in a weed-choked bed,
scrap of paper scrawled with what the doctor said.

Those seeded crackers we ate with lobster salad that time.
Your lost earring. Your friend from junior high, online.

And finding you—a miracle. What are the odds?
I find myself on my knees. Weeding, thanking God.

WOMAN COMES INTO THE BAR

A woman comes into the bar where I work, asks me how her hair looks. Fussing
in the bar mirror, right of the Ardbeg, left of Lagavulin. Her bangs don't match her
extensions, and I agree with my father: only floozies dye their hair. But I lie. She's on
something, says there's two warrants out for her arrest, and some asshole just stole all
her stuff. *My woman stuff, you know what I mean?* I don't know what she means.

She means her makeup. She's glad she looks okay. She only has ten dollars. It's a
nice bar, but we have five-dollar wine on tap, which isn't so nice, no matter what my
manager says. It's terrible, unless you're spending your last ten bucks on wine. If so,
I'll fill your cup to the top. She grabs hold of my hand, touches my ring like she just
found it, her long lost ring, her own.

She asks, *How old do you think I am?* I pretend I'm thinking it over, look at her face,
appraising, like I'm going to tell the truth. Twenty-six, I lie. Good answer. Then she
takes another gulp of wine and sobs: what a terrible day. No way to Waltham, two
warrants, her good makeup, her flat iron, going to jail…

I am not interested in makeup. I am interested in jail. *Have you been to Framingham?*
I ask her. She stops crying, tilts her head. I tell her if she ends up there, there's lots
of great girls, and cosmetology classes. *And, plus: you can't take your stuff to jail
anyway! So who needs all that stuff? Not you.* I make her laugh. She drinks her wine.
She tells me she'll see me in jail.

THE WOMEN IN THE SHOE STORE ADS ARE ALL IN LOVE WITH EACH OTHER, BUT NOT REALLY THEY ARE IN LOVE WITH SHOES THOUSANDS OF SHOES

I write this on a scrap of paper, leave it by the TV for weeks.
Next time I see the ad, I stop, rewind, watch the commercial

twenty times. I'd never go into a shoe store that big, but I recognize
desire. Sly, sexy music; great deals; no men. Endless lunches,

lattes, enormous dressing rooms, your caress of your friend's gleaming shoulder,
your beautiful friend laughing, leaning in to whisper in slow

motion in your ear. The price of a pair your passport: all races, every age.
Sundresses of coral, lapis. Huge eyes bashful with need, the need

to share. Legs now flung into the air: *Look, my dear, dear friend,
the women say, look at my glossy bare legs, the brand new shoes I got*

on sale. Meaningful sidelong glances, eyes bright with singular bargains,
   secured.
And shoes. More shoes, great deals on shoes. Thousands and thousands of
   shoes.

TWO WHITE WOMEN WALK INTO A BANK

We were two white women at a desk in a bank.
Behind the desk, a black woman bank notary, Bianca,
sorted and stamped all the papers we signed, proof
of our worth, worth the risk of a loan. She said she'd never
seen so many forms required, so many years' worth
of taxes, so many proofs of so many jobs. *It's because
we're both ladies*, I shrugged. Bianca blinked. *Racist*, she
said, and we took half a second, all laughed together out loud.

ROOM FOR PARTY

Make room for party. Make way for baby. *HELL*
YEAH my sweater says with a skull that's what
happens when you get drunk at lunch in Montreal
and then go shopping HELL YEAH. Make room
for yes. The dim sum place by Dumpling Café has it
both ways. *Empire Garden* says one side of its marquee;
Emperor Garden the other. So it hides, even though
it's enormous: an old vaudeville theatre, complete
with proscenium, murals, gold everywhere, gold
dragon and crane with red lights for eyes, seven-
dollar scorpion bowls, synchronized squads of ladies
with their carts of chicken feet, shrimp noodle, chive
dumpling, beef ball. We love it. They advertise ROOM
FOR PARTY, which we take in, co-opt, say *I have*
room for party, you? You always have room
for party. I think I have a little room left for party.
I'm tired. No room for party. Get a room, let's party.
You don't need much room for party. Josey and I
on the 39 coming home from a date, making out
on the bus, in the car wash—*You two still make out?*
asks Nellie. Hell Yeah, Nellie—cracking each
other up in the aisle—no room for two middle-aged
ladies to sit. And then the babydyke, her earnest haircut,
sweet round face, said, *You two are so inspiring*,
toddle-swaggered off the bus. In our father's
mansion there are so many rooms for party: 1. 7. 45.

IN WHICH I AM ACCUSED OF SLEEPING MY WAY TO THE TOP

In other news, this is the top. Weep for what little things
would make them jealous. I publish a poem

online, and people post comments. Smart little analyses, short papers
they might turn in for school. Or "This is not a good poem. Here's

a good poem." Then they post their poems. One man posts a photo
of my face, says *Look at her; obviously she's fucking the editor.* Fucking!

The editor! To publish a sonnet about an execution. Look at that face!
This one! The face of a whore. There is a backlash, back and forth

over my slutty face, lecherous editors. The man
apologizes for going too far. My face is still up there, though,

with comments about how slutty I look. I am in my thirties
in the picture. It looks like me. No makeup. A student

evaluation once included this sentence: *Sometimes I think Jill
forgets to brush her hair.* This is sexy. This is all that. I am ecstatic.

Those eyes I thought were tired? In truth, they smolder. Those lips,
a little chapped? Come hither. The bags under my eyes

have bags. I hoped I looked a little wise, projected empathy.
I forget that I'm a woman, that for some people that's enough.

SHIFTING FAITH

I'm driving again, belted, locked in tight. It's late.
I'm safe, driving past schoolyards and prisons,
fenced in identical fence. Insiders, outsiders,
open windows. Doors closed as faces. Past rivers,
package stores, county lines, redemption centers.
Into time zones, icy patches, new states, riots of blossoming trees.
This is me. I'm driving, reckless, past signs I could read
but don't. Don't know the speed limit, don't
know the name of this town with the diner,
sign outside saying LUNCH
AND INNER SPECIALS quietly,
to itself. *Inner specials? I'm not even near*
her specials, I say to the windshield, the steering wheel,
merging, signaling, pulling tight
into a space. *Rectum? Damn near killed 'em*
I murmur to odometer, gearshift, emergency and
you, dear reader: somewhere, inside, emerging,
I know you know what I mean.

It's always open. I leave my own upholstery, walk inside,
ask to hear the inner specials. The waitress smiles, forgives, her
lined green *ORDERS* pad held in one hand, her pen a benediction.
She gazes upward, inward. She recites, glowing.
The words cross into my inner ear, become: Faith.
The Body. Home. This is not a joke. Or it is, maybe,
to you, never to the waitress. She means. She works
so hard to tell us, to please. Every table's different.
Needing refills, second helpings, saying grace.
She is tired, so tired, eyelids dark as labia,
eyelids darker than lips.

SEWN STRIPES, EMBROIDERED STARS

After the election, once McCain had conceded and Josey bought a round
of Rittenhouse for the bar, after we stumbled into the ladies' room

at the Independent for necking, crying, then rode back home with Bob and
    Chelsea
in Rose Marie's car, honking and hollering *OBAMA! OBAMA!* out the
    windows

to assembled crowds of happy Americans all the way across town, we watched
our TiVoed election coverage, drank Seelbachs, crashed, woke up and bought
a flag.

We went online and bought a flag. 100% cotton, made in America, *sewn
stripes, embroidered stars*. A flagpole, a flagpole bracket. I had never bought a
flag,

worried with the vague remembered worry from Girl Scouts about how to fold
the flag, when to bring it down, but Josey said *We'll keep our porch light on it.*

*It's cotton, so it's going to fade and get a little speckled with mildew, a little
tattered over the winter. It's going to be beautiful. We'll never take it down.*

SONNET FOR THE MONEY

How quickly we turn from grateful to greedy.
—Ann Patchett

Everybody knows money can turn it all around.
Cover rent, school loans, groceries, everything we require—
we find fresh needs: wooden bowls. A trip into town.
Puny humans, our adorable desires.
When I won that big check I asked for the cash;
I wanted to smell it, thumb the crisp heft
that changed my life. They put it in my hands.
Fat stacks of twenties on the bank manager's desk, left
alone with all our dreams come true. What changed?
I took pictures of my overflowing purse,
held more money in my arms than I made
most years. Remembered debt, jobs, worry, worse,
and felt relief like *that*. The money counter whirred.
We watched, talked about lunch. Started to get bored.

POOR PUSSY

Carl says he wants to open a door
in Ed's chest and crawl in, which makes us fall

in love with Carl. We want to be near
him, stand too close

in bars. Carl makes us want to play
Poor Pussy, a parlor game we learned when we

were five. My grandma taught me. You
can look it up. You keep a straight face

while someone pets your head and says
poor pussy. Poor, poor pussy. Or

at least you try. I am a Poor Pussy
champion, want Carl to lose to me

again and again. Come back, Carl,
we love you. Carl, we'll let you win.

GAY FREAKING ASSHOLES: ON TOLERANCE

For Skip Horack

When I was teaching writing camp with Skip,
we both pretended that we had the skills
to teach teenagers. Easy enough with smart kids.
Psyched for free lunch—cafeteria-grilled
organic chicken from farms with fancy names
like *The Happy Clucker*: *Jenny's Farm in the Pines*.
Oh, Jenny. We sat happy with our trays
of tacos, soft serve, teasing. And then one time
we overheard one kid call another *a gay
freaking asshole*. We froze, tried not to laugh.
Real teachers wouldn't tolerate intolerance. They'd
say *Tolerance. Language. Bullying. Or Shut Your Trap*:
who knows. They'd trade fun lunch for a talk, kids' tears.

We call each other *gay freaking asshole* for years.

SEALING WOODROW

My parents visit me in Salt Lake City
and we go let the Mormons tell us who
we are, or who we've been. Museum
of names of the dead they keep: the Granite
Mountain Records Vault, huge caves with Mosler doors.
The missionaries are adorable, girls from Argentina,
Brazil. I say they're welcome to baptize our dead
once we figure out who they are. I think I'm really
funny. I think it's a myth, a stereotype: matzoh
made with Christian blood, Muslims blowing
stuff up. But no—one thanks me, reassures me
the dead *have agency*, that nobody can force
you, dead or alive, to believe anything you don't.
Our dead can decide; she'll just give them a chance.
Later, when my dad gives me crap for pimping my
forefathers out, I see a pair of earnest, suited angels
on bikes, missionaries knocking on my
grandpa Woodrow's cloud. They wake him up.
What I remember most of my grandfather: him
saying *pipe down*, telling me *go cut a switch*.
He was kidding. Hey, Gonka: here's what you get.
Eternal pitch, days of scripture, winged
boys on bikes waving their golden plates and saying
our family will be sealed together forever. Forever:
he could barely stand me during half time, little me
dancing in the smoke from his Salems by his scratchy
La-Z-Boy, his thumb in his hollow of cheek. They'll preach
till he gets the picture, knows the truth: I became
the pain in the ass he always knew I'd be, there's
an afterlife, he's in it, and I'm thinking of him.

PERFECT HAPPINESS

The Nantucket ferry in its cream
of brackish harbor ice. Thickish slabs of ice,
awkward, heavy, rising slowly on the swell
of water. The open water, behind them, thick
and smooth as taffy, stirred by the heavy prop.

Perfect happiness was in the ferry from
Nantucket, churning the thick water with
its skin of breaking ice, and on her bike,
the first girl off the ferry, the fifth

of January, 2001. The quick press of riding
from the harbor, and then the warm truck.
Gloves off, Bobby Short on public radio.
Still thinking she was coming home to you.

OUR FATHER

A year or two, mornings before school,
our father came into our rooms with pliers.
My sisters and I crammed into Jordache
casings, Gloria Vanderbilts. We'd jump
into jeans, tug them up our ashy thighs, abrade
young skin with denim seams. Taut denimed butts
on polyester Holly Hobbie bedspreads, until they
were painted on, until our arms ached, our fingers
hurt, until we were panting, exhausted, our smooth
foreheads beaded with sweat. Near tears as usual,
calling for help. After the first time, when he laughed
but then couldn't grip the brass zipper, so ha ha dad
the joke's on you, he kept pliers handy, grabbed
the pull tab, tugged it up the teeth so we
could button our own damn pants. What we think
we want. What we know. What do we know
when we ask for what we think we want? We pray
for ridiculous things, we humans. And so often are indulged.

SATAN'S CUPBOARD

A morning with Athena,
the Boston Athenaeum's online catalog.

An afternoon with Mary, Assistant Reference Librarian. She points
out heads of the dead: hidden relief of Dante, hooded

Petrarch, dusty Shakespeare in the stairwell. *On your right,*
here's Jesus Christ; on the left you've got your Satan. Christ:

huge with grace, forbearance, years across the hall
from Beelzebub. *He's looking down on us*, says Mary, who should know.

I stoop, and see his placid brow is hairless. Lucifer's
is out of bounds, unruly eyebrows of an old professor, cast out

by his wife. His line of sight is blocked by the King's Chapel Collection,
stately cupboard of books. Satan sneers, has always sneered,

at *Keith's Dispute with Quakers, Illustrations of More, Defences of More.*
During the renovations, he saw less than ever: dim interior of crate. Forgive

his bitterness: the prince of the power of air's now carved in marble. All
this knowledge hanging, ripe, just out of reach. His chin cleft or cloven, hair

corkscrewed, tumbling forth
like a fountain, like

Athena herself from the forehead of Zeus. Mary says that during renovations
the cupboard's shelves were misplaced, lost

a long time. *Where did they turn up?* I ask. She intercedes, asks
Stanley. Satan, that old serpent, hid them under prints and portfolios,

under power of darkness. Untidy spirit, spiteful on the return of the bookshelves, books that Satan looks at: *More on Apocalypse, Sherlock*

on Death, Goodman on Sin. Lucifer, on his pedestal,
is tempered by these neighbors, through with acquisitions. He would kill

to be their editor. He could suggest a few changes, hopeful
new titles in the tradition of *Fowler on Christian Liberty*,

Stillingfleet on the Separation,
Defence of Snake in the Grass.

MAN'S MAN

A ladies' man is often
a man's man, Thomas
points out, and we see
how far this can go.
He points at Sarah, says
She's a real woman's
woman, which makes
her sound kind
of gay. Woman's woman:
gay. Man's man? Couldn't
be straighter. *Mano*
a mano or *man to man*.
We talk about this
over burgers, drink
our beers. Three
people, a vinyl
booth, a heart
to heart. A *tête-à-tête*.

LATE LEEKS

For Linda Mikula

Linda arrives with the leeks to end all leeks,
direct from her garden, practically hydroponic,
flawless, already creamy, pale
and perfect in an enormous bundle, sturdy
as a homecoming bouquet, held in one arm
like a sheaf of wheat, a dozen dozen roses, their
size and heft amazing, even for leeks.
When I slice them open their creamy centers
are pale and pefect. Flick them like pages
in a book with your thumb—dirt-free,
blank pages, ready for any recipe you want,
vichyssoise, potato leek, any gratin, braise or stew
but we make creamed leeks for Thanksgiving;
thank you, Linda. We're thanking Linda for the leeks.

JOSEY PACKS A BOX

Roughneck Rubbermaid tote filled with flea market
finds: fifties casseroles, Pyrex refrigerator stacks.
Old-fashioned Old Fashioned glasses, silver rims etched
with daffodils. Tin camping cups with speckled
blue enamel. She wraps each item in my sweaters,
doesn't make fun of the Waldorf Park City toilet
paper I stole to make her laugh. *It makes good
packing material*, she says. Layers of vintage
dish towels. Tin cups filled with selenium, those
glass-looking rocks. She's taking all my treasures
home with her. In the hours before we are ripped
apart again, she packs for me while I drink coffee,
look at her, her ripped arms and thoughtful brow,
vow we'll never part again. *I just found your nightgown,
so I bet my pants are in here somewhere*, she says,
patting my folded jeans before she puts them away.

GIN AND TONIC, CITRUS, JIFFY POP

Evenings cool with opalescent gin
and tonics, the silver globe heating,
unfurling, expanding, the not-Doppler
of the popping rising up then popping out.

The apartment had beige carpet, ceiling-white
walls. A sort of bachelor pad for me, visiting
for Spring Term. I made the same grocery list
again and again: *Gin and Tonic. Citrus. Jiffy Pop.*

It's pathetic what little things can make me glad.
Each day up at noon, trying to get anything fresh done
in the face of the endless in-box, hacking at it like weeds
in the abandoned Air Force base. I'd try to turn off

the wifi, afraid to turn my back for long. I thought
of a children's book, its magic kettle filled with stew
when the righteous were hungry, silverware to sell
when they were full. And when the bad ones stole

it, the little kettle filled with mud, filled
their whole house with stony mud up to the windows,
drowned them in it. I remember the grit in my mouth
in my bed, fear of mud sealing in my ears.

Not that I compare myself to them, the bad ones.
My frivolous problems, popcorn suppers. Day
after day of the email, the everyday, and the small.

DR. LI SHOVELS!

It was the winter I lost the best
job, and the truck broke, and the ceiling
fell in. Winter of debt, injector pumps, horse-
hair plaster dusting everything we owned. It was
the day I got stuck in the square, wasted
day I could've spent at home with plaster,
joint tape, perforated ceiling washers,
compound, drywall screws. I *love*
drywall screws, an inch
and five eights, five pound boxes.
Dark smudge on my fingers, pulling plaster
home to lath.

December: already sick
of slush, December's banks of dirty snows,
picking my way across obscured curbs, slick
streets, I heard your voice
via voice mail, a message
reporting you'd shoveled the driveway, pulled in the truck.
I love you, and I've been thinking. I think you
should buy some champagne, because we're rich.

Rich. In seconds, I stopped fantasizing about calling
in sick. I bought Cardullo's cheapest sparkling wine,
and soon I had my students laughing, writing
wintertime haiku:

Dr. Li shovels!
Wow! Moving the Great Walls here.
Miracles in snow.

BRUEGEL

Trying to say *Breugel* I say *Broogle*, not
Broygle, rhyme with *Google,* not *oy, girl.*

I blush, remember I'm from French Broad Elementary School
in Alexander, North Carolina. Not that Bruegel himself

would recognize we're calling his name. On a train outside of Brugge
I heard a conductor laugh when my dad said *Bruggie*

in his soft Peoria-to-Alexander accent, and I thought *Look,*
you Belgian a-hole, come back to Alexander, try to say <u>Alexander</u>

<u>*Missionary Baptist Church*</u>, say *y'uns*, say *y'all*, say *saved.* I'm
the pedantic one now, tell people to say *guzzle* not *ghaZAHL*, although

ghaZAHL sounds classier. But Shahid, (not ShaHEED) said it right, taught
me what to say. I said *unwieldly* for forty years: there's no reason

to be a dick. A student calls a *ghazal* a *gazelle*, gets embarrassed.
But I prefer it, say *know what? I'ma start saying that, too.*

THE WHOLE HOUSE LOOKED BETTER WHEN GODFREY WAS IN IT

We didn't know him from Adam, the lanky man
in Prada lighting up our rooms with class
and action. A charming Irishman. With him
in the house I dreamt of a magic car, sleek
black roadster with leather steering wheel, leather
buttons that shifted its shape—Town Car to Mercedes
to Navigator, Porsche Boxster, all of them gleaming
meanly through greenly lit tunnels to airports in countries
at night. Kanji blurred to Gaelic on the road signs:
the Mass Pike pilgrim hat transformed
to thatched roof, to golden Buddha. A great dream.

Prada has a fabric that travels
beautifully; Godfrey took handfuls of his suit
to crumple, show us how the lines
stay lean and navy. His belt—reversible, Hermès—
cost more than all my shoes, heaped in a sterling
laundry bin. Our martinis passed his muster: our
man Godfrey reclined on our chaise, took it
from lounge to *longue*.

In the morning, hungover, he took his time tying
his sleek leather boots, put down
his bag to open his arms and hold us, tell us
his place in Manhattan is small, but we're welcome, and
in Paris he has a spare room. *Paris, then*, we said,
discerningly; he nodded, didn't mention
our matching flannel plaid pajamas, bare feet. Our
boozy morning faces without makeup, our street too rough
for him to park on. Our old house, glamour already
fading as he put his Longchamp bag in the cab.

FERRIS WHEEL'S A SHIP

My freshmen write sentences using apostrophes
to indicate possession, and one girl writes
Ferris wheel's a ship. This is the same girl
who said *There was balls up there*
when asked why she climbed to the roof.
I'm in Utah. I'm a visiting writer. I need
to explain why *Ferris wheel's a ship* is not a good use
of apostrophes, but I just love it so much I don't care.

I stand at the board thinking of Mr. Ferris Wheel, a
person, who is just crazy. That Ferris: a ship, a storm
himself, a whirling dervish out of hand. Freewheeling
Ferris! Or no, she's quoting an invented laconic farmer,
unnamed, who looks wisely up at the meddling agent outside
the local fair. Too late! The whole town has already
gotten together to help the lovable alien escape. Might as well
tell the city slicker how the little guy got away.

Ferris. Wheel's. A Ship, I say, pausing, so they know
they're in trouble. *Ferris Wheel's a Ship was the name
of my band in high school,* I say. *Really?* they say. *No.*

EIGHT OF WANDS

You will be able to do pretty much whatever you want without any
restrictions or holdups.
—Teach Me Tarot website

Wanting wands, wants, granting eight wantings
wanting whatever you want. Don't I know it. Ain't it
the truth. All of us around here pretty much able to do
pretty much what we want. Pretty good news,
Hard Work Paying Off. Sweet, *Haste, Hurry, Rush,*
Race. What privilege tastes like—more. The luxury
of wanting; *make me want it* a bonus, since most
of us are stuck just wanting more. When the hardest part
is figuring out what you want, you know you have it
pretty good: stop wanting. Or at least stop whining;
dude, you're already there. Top of the heap! Best
of both worlds, buster! Cream of the crop dusters! Stop
fussing, start making nice things for somebody else.
You can have nice things. So can we. You're all set! Set
for life. Must be nice. It must be nice. If you lived here
you'd be home now! And here you are, safe at home.
When they *I've heard so much about you* I used to say
the thing you say: *All good I hope!* Har har. Now I
get right down to it, brass tacks, all business, now I
just nod, say *good.* Now I am able to do pretty much
whatever I want without any restrictions or holdups.
So here's what I want: what you want. Helping
you. How can I help you? Tell me. Tell me what you want.

WHAT'S NEW

I work on an essay about the New South, hear
Josey talking to Siri in the next room. Josey's
drinking coffee and texting Adam, using a robot voice
to say it's. *Def-in-ite-ly. A New World. Period*, trying
to help Siri understand. Siri understands. She's
texting Adam about trans stuff, what happens to young
butches when everybody's trans. Everybody: as if.
So what's new? I imagine butches never imagined
pressure from the left. Too busy with douches like
Santorum, his man-on-dog, how once gays get married,
what keeps people from fucking their dogs? Oh,
Rick, poor Rick; no one wants to fuck a dog but you,
dude. Dudes snort at Rachel, say she looks like a man:
Wait, what's wrong with looking like a man? I ask.
I thought we all liked men. I love me my fellow man.
Going trans—like IVF, or getting a puppy—just seems
like a lot of hassle to me. Lucky me: life so finely tuned
that something new just seems too much, too much to do,
too much trouble to have to go through. Washing dishes,
making slow cooker beef stew's enough for me. Josey goes
across the street, new condo's open house, texts to tell me,
Siri-free. *Tell me if you can see me from in there*, I ask,
wondering if we need better blinds. I see people inside,
in their baseball hats, imagining new lives, new walk to their
new subway stop. People slowly turning through fresh
new rooms, all of them wanting to live across from us.
High noon, streets sloppy with old snow. Power lines
twitch off their cold and glassy rain. New footsteps walk up
the new stairs across the street, again and again and again.

RECENT TITLES FROM ALICE JAMES BOOKS

To the Wren: Collected & New Poems, Jane Mead
Angel Bones, Ilyse Kusnetz
Monsters I Have Been, Kenji C. Liu
Soft Science, Franny Choi
Bicycle in a Ransacked City: An Elegy, Andrés Cerpa
Anaphora, Kevin Goodan
Ghost, like a Place, Iain Haley Pollock
Isako Isako, Mia Ayumi Malhotra
Of Marriage, Nicole Cooley
The English Boat, Donald Revell
We, the Almighty Fires, Anna Rose Welch
DiVida, Monica A. Hand
pray me stay eager, Ellen Doré Watson
Some Say the Lark, Jennifer Chang
Calling a Wolf a Wolf, Kaveh Akbar
We're On: A June Jordan Reader, Edited by Christoph Keller and Jan Heller Levi
Daylily Called It a Dangerous Moment, Alessandra Lynch
Surgical Wing, Kristin Robertson
The Blessing of Dark Water, Elizabeth Lyons
Reaper, Jill McDonough
Madwoman, Shara McCallum
Contradictions in the Design, Matthew Olzmann
House of Water, Matthew Nienow
World of Made and Unmade, Jane Mead
Driving without a License, Janine Joseph
The Big Book of Exit Strategies, Jamaal May
play dead, francine j. harris
Thief in the Interior, Phillip B. Williams
Second Empire, Richie Hofmann
Drought-Adapted Vine, Donald Revell
Refuge/es, Michael Broek
O'Nights, Cecily Parks
Yearling, Lo Kwa Mei-en
Sand Opera, Philip Metres
Devil, Dear, Mary Ann McFadden

Alice James Books is committed to publishing books that matter. The press was founded in 1973 in Boston, Massachusetts as a cooperative, wherein authors performed the day-to-day undertakings of the press. This element remains present today, as authors who publish with the press are invited to collaborate closely in the publication process of their work. AJB remains committed to its founders' original feminist mission, while expanding upon the scope to include all voices and poets who might otherwise go unheard. In keeping with its efforts to build equity and increase inclusivity in publishing and the literary arts, AJB seeks out poets whose writing possesses the range, depth, and ability to cultivate empathy in our world and to dynamically push against silence. The press was named for Alice James, sister to William and Henry, whose extraordinary gift for writing went unrecognized during her lifetime.

Designed by Anna Reich
annareichdesign

Printed by McNaughton & Gunn